Money
Matters

Ariennir yn Rhannol gan
Lywodraeth Cymru
Part Funded by
Welsh Government

Ariennir yn rhannol gan Lywodraeth Cymru fel rhan o'i
rhaglen gomisiynu adnoddau addysgu a dysgu Cymraeg
a dwyieithog

Part funded by the Welsh Government as part of its
Welsh and bilingual teaching and learning resources
commissioning programme

Justin The-Way

by Gwenno Mair Davies

illustrated by Rhiannon Sparks

Justin couldn't believe his luck, and he couldn't
believe his eyes either. He closed his eyes and rubbed
them, before opening them again. No, it wasn't his
imagination playing tricks with him! There, hiding in the
shadow of the pavement on the side of the road was a
... pound coin!

This was a great discovery for someone like
Justin because he was a keen coin collector. He aimed
to collect ten pence a day. He would look for coins

under the tables in the school hall at lunchtime and between paving slabs on his way home from school. He would look down the arm of the sofa at home in the evenings. People could be so careless with their money, especially coins, but you'd never hear Justin complaining about that.

Justin was enough of a mathematician to know that, if he collected a penny every day, he could get £3.65 by the end of the year. But by collecting *ten pence* a day, he could collect *ten times* as much! Imagine how much money he could make like this in a year if he came across a *pound* every day! And in ten years … he could be as rich as the head teacher!

Yes, his classmates made fun of him every time they saw him jumping for joy after finding a penny on the playing field. But Justin was used to that. After all, they made fun of him for so many things. Things like the fact that he liked coming to school. Things like the fact that his trousers were so short and hovered about ten centimetres from the floor. And things like the fact that the sleeves of his jumper did not reach much further than his elbows.

Not forgetting, of course, all the teasing because of his name. That was to be expected, probably, ever since the day he was born when his mother had named him Justin The-Way Jones.

Justin picked up the pound coin and examined it. He liked reading the words of the national anthem,

'Pleidiol wyf i'm gwlad', around the edge of the Welsh pound. He gave the coin a big triumphant kiss before tucking it safely in the left pocket of his school trousers. (There wasn't a hole in that one, unlike his right pocket.)

So no, life wasn't easy for poor Justin The-Way Jones. Life wasn't easy at school or at home where he lived in poverty with his mean mother and her harsh words. But Justin had a dream, that one day he would be a success. And he was getting closer to the key to his success every day, with every penny he found.

He slowed his steps as he passed the window of Shop Around. This was the kind of bric-a-brac store that every town has, selling all kinds of junk, from second-hand toothbrushes to packs of tinned dinosaur food. But there, in the middle of all the jumble, was the treasure he longed for; the treasure which would bring him closer to success.

'One day, you will be mine,' he whispered through the glass to the huge green book with the large gold letters which spelled 'WOW WORDS!'. The book - a dictionary - sat proudly in the centre of the shop window, stuffed between an old rag doll with a missing eye, and a set of false teeth in a glass of water.

The first step in Justin's journey to success was buying this dictionary. He wanted to learn lots of new, long words, ready for when the time came for him to go to secondary school. So, this was going to be his first purchase and his first investment with the money he had already begun to save. Since the first day of September, Justin had managed to collect ten pence a day, except for this day, the first of October, when he'd found a pound! He worked out that he was halfway to collecting enough money to buy the dictionary. That was much sooner than expected!

Justin wiped away the condensation, which had formed in a circle on the window from his breath as he pressed against the glass, to admire the book again. As he did so, he noticed a bright yellow star-shaped card, lying upside down by the dictionary. He tried to read the writing on it, but that was quite a challenge without standing on his head!

Justin was pretty sure that the words written in the

SHOP AROUND

star read: 'HALF PRICE!' He was even more certain that the star was meant to be stuck on the dictionary. If that was true, today would be the best day ever! After all, between the pound in his pocket and the loose change locked in his piggy bank in his bedroom, he would have enough money to buy it!

2

Simon, the shopkeeper, nearly jumped out of his skin when the bell rang above Shop Around's door. He'd forgotten how loud the noise was, because he couldn't remember the last time someone had called into his shop.

He pushed his half-moon, thick-lensed glasses closer to his narrow eyes to get a better view of the rare thing that stood before him ... a 'customer'.

'Hmm, it's one of those young ones,' he thought,

and he screwed up his nose. Shop Around Simon had no patience with children or young people ever since that time in 2010 when a few of them had come in, one after the other, to ask for ridiculous things which didn't exist – just as a dare.

'I wanted to ask you about …' Justin had no chance to finish his sentence.

'Before you ask, I don't sell glass hammers, elbow grease, tartan paint or buckets of fresh air in this shop,' said Simon, abruptly.

'But …'

'So, you and your friends can go and laugh at some other shop owner, because I'm not going to fall into that trap again.' The fact that he had wasted many minutes searching his storeroom for those items back in 2010 had clearly left a deep mark on Simon.

'Huh! Children!' he mumbled under his breath, before clearing his throat to declare, 'When I was your age …'

'The dictionary in the window.' It was Justin's turn to interrupt this time. His voice was strong. 'Is there a half price discount on it?'

The silence meant that he had managed to gain Simon's attention. Simon studied Justin carefully, from head to toe, and back up to his forehead again.

'Yes, but for one day only. Tomorrow, it will be back to its original price, which is eight pounds …'

'I'll buy it. Today!' Justin announced, with a

wide grin on his pleased face. He thought he saw a glimmer of a smile on the shop owner's face too, as he shook his bald head. The old man couldn't believe he was finally going to sell something!

Grumbling and groaning, Simon went to the window and stretched over the old church organ, past the scarecrow made from empty cans of baked beans, and grabbed *Wow Words!* Slowly and carefully he lifted the big heavy book, but nearly dropped it again when he heard the doorbell's deafening ring for the second time that day ... that year even. But nobody entered the shop this time. It was ringing because someone had left. He could see the scruffy looking boy through the window, pointing down the street.

'I'm just going to get the money!' mimed Justin on the other side of the window. Then he turned on his heel and rushed towards home, leaving Simon standing open-mouthed in his shop window.

Every step of his way home, words swirled through Justin's head. They were common old words, overused by everyone. Soon, however, he would never have to use these again. No, he would have new words – words he didn't even know existed yet. Words from the dictionary which he could shoot at the nasty children in the school playground, and insult them without them knowing what the words meant.

Soon, he reached the street where he lived. Ahead, he could see the building which was more of a house than a home to him. Justin sprinted through the crooked gate hanging lazily on one hinge, along the concrete path around the corner towards the back door.

Then it was time for him to be quiet. He didn't want his mother to hear that he was home, or he would have to make up an excuse so that he could go back out to the shop again. He could hear his mother howling along to a song blasting from the radio in the lounge. She wasn't singing the right words, or the right notes either, come to that. But Justin had more important things to worry about. He tiptoed through the kitchen, along the hallway, holding his breath as he passed the open door of the lounge.

'La, la, la ...' sang Mam in her hoarse voice, as Justin climbed the stairs, three steps at a time.

At the top of the stairs, he turned to stand in front of the door of his bedroom. All he needed to do now was grab his piggy bank off the windowsill, and retrace his steps back to Shop Around. Slowly and deliberately, he opened the door just enough for him squeeze his body through the gap, and avoid the squeaking sound the door usually made when it was open halfway. Success!

Justin turned his attention towards the window, to his piggy bank. But it wasn't there. Not in the form of the pig he was expecting to see anyway. Instead, there were only large, sharp shards of broken pottery, and a lonely two pence coin lurking beneath the piece which was once the little pig's nose.

'Nooooo!' cried Justin, falling to the floor with his head in his hands, trying, unsuccessfully, to prevent his tears from flowing.

*   *   *

Back in Shop Around, Simon too was shaking his head, unable to believe that once again, he had been tricked by a child.

3

At that exact moment, in the silence between two songs on the radio, Justin's mum heard the sound from the room above – Justin's bedroom. A sound like something, or someone, falling to the floor. With her glossy magazine nestling in her lap, she snorted an irritated sigh and eyed the ceiling. Who or what on earth had the nerve to draw her attention away from her precious 'radio and magazine time'? She placed her magazine carefully on the table by her chair before taking off one slipper, in case she needed a weapon. Then, with heavy steps, she climbed up the stairs.

SCREEEECH!! The door complained as it was hurled wide open. Justin's mother strode in and saw Justin sitting on the floor, his head in his hands.

'Oh, it's you!' she snapped. 'I was beginning to think that we had a burglar in the house.'

She was about to return to her beloved radio and magazine, when she heard Justin say under his breath, 'You're right, there is a burglar in the house.'

'What did you say?' She looked fiercely at her son, only to see him looking steadily back at her, his eyes red and puffy.

'Someone stole my money,' he said, looking straight into his mother's eyes.

'No one has stolen anything. I *borrowed* your money.'

'Borrowing means I'll get it back,' ventured Justin, trying his best to hold the tears back.

'Oh, you'll get your money back all right!' His mother was shouting by now, as she ploughed through her pockets, searching for something. 'You'll get your money back in the supper you'll eat tonight, boyo.'

She'd found the thing she was looking for. A receipt from the Corner Shop. She held the piece of paper out and stuffed it under Justin's nose.

'Putting food on the table is an expensive job,

Justin, and it's only right for you to contribute to the cost of living from time to time.'

'But,' Justin tried to explain as tears ran down his cheeks. 'I was saving the money to buy a dictionary, to learn new words ...'

'A dictionary?!' shouted his mother. 'A DICTIONARY?!' she screeched. Her face turned red as she spat the words from her mouth: 'Can you eat a dictionary for supper? Can you wrap yourself in it to keep warm? Grow up, Justin. And if you want to learn new words, why not learn these: Money ... does ... not ... grow ... on ... trees!'

And with that, she tore the receipt in her hand

The Corner Shop

potatoes   £1.50
bread   £0.80
baked beans £0.75
magazine   £3.50

and threw the two halves up into the air. Then, she marched out of the room and slammed the door shut behind her.

Both pieces of paper fell like confetti, the biggest piece gently landing on Justin's lap.

He wiped his eyes with his sleeve, and used the other sleeve to wipe his nose. He opened his fist to reveal the two pence piece he had managed to save from his mother. Yes, he'd been hurt, and had lost a month's worth of savings, but he was not going to let this shatter his dream. If anything, this unfortunate event had strengthened his resolve. He reached into his left pocket for the pound he had found that day. He had £1.02, and all he needed now was a good place to hide the coins, safe and secure.

Feeling even more determined to succeed, Justin stood up and scanned his bedroom. Under the bed? In the socks and underpants drawer? Under his pillow? No, no, no. There was no point hiding them in his room. They would not be safe there or in any other room in the house from his mother's thieving hands. Looking for inspiration, he stared out of the window. Justin stared through his own reflection and noticed next door's small dog digging in the garden. It had a bone to bury.

'Come on, Justin! Think!' he muttered to himself, turning his attention back and forth from his sad reflection to next door's dog hiding his treasured belonging.

Of course! The answer was there, in front of him! He could learn a valuable lesson from the little dog next door and bury his money in the ground!

Later that night, while his mother was in her weekly line dancing class, Justin was busy digging and burying his money in an old sock in the ground. Aunty Brenda had come over to keep an eye on him. (She wasn't a real aunt, or any relation, just a friend of his mother with whom she played Bingo every Friday night.) But since she'd arrived, she'd barely raised her head from her Sudoku puzzle book, and had hardly noticed what Justin had been up to.

Justin stood by the back door of the house to look at the garden and admire his work. He had done such a great job of levelling the ground after all the digging work, he himself could not point to the exact spot where the money was hidden.

However, that wasn't a problem for him as he had a system to find the exact spot. It wasn't a map,

17

because his mum might find the map and locate his
treasure. He had to be smarter than that. No, he had
created his own verse (and learned it off by heart) so
that he could know where exactly to find his sock of
wealth:

> *How many seconds are there in a minute?*
> *How many minutes in an hour?*
> *How many days in one whole week?*
> *Add the total all together.*
> *Take away from this one hundred,*
> *Along with the number of months in a year.*
> *Calculate and then you measure,*
> *'Cause my treasure's hidden here.*

All Justin needed to do was count that total number of steps as he walked one foot after the other carefully in a straight line from the back door. Then, he should land on the exact spot where the money was buried!

'JUSTIN THE-WAY JONES!' thundered Aunty Brenda's voice. Her long face with its thin, pointed nose poked through the open kitchen window. 'You'll catch your death out there in the garden, with it being so cold. And talking of cold things – get yourself into the house, your beans on toast have been on the kitchen table for a good while!'

5

Justin woke up suddenly, a few minutes before it was time for his ridiculously loud alarm clock to go off. He'd had a nightmare. He'd dreamed that his mother had turned into a great big mole, and was digging through the ground in the garden, until the house was buried under a large molehill. He knew that the mole, was, in fact, his mother because its face was just like hers. But the face was on the body of a mole, with two large hands shovelling their way through the soil. Aunty Brenda was there too, laughing and shouting instructions, 'To the right! Right! Left a bit ...'

'The money!' thought Justin suddenly, before leaping out of bed and running to the window. He took a deep breath before he opened the curtains, expecting the worst. But the soil hadn't been turned at all. It hadn't been touched since he was there last night, digging. And yet, *something* was different. He stared at a small tree, about a metre high, which looked quite lonely and sad in the garden. He was pretty sure he hadn't seen that tree there before. And it was very close to the point where he had buried the sock of money. But that couldn't be right, surely ...?

Justin tiptoed quickly but quietly down the stairs. He grabbed his coat from the back of a chair in the kitchen and rushed out into the garden, barefoot. He recited the verse to remember how many steps he needed to take, before measuring, one foot after the other. One ... two ... three ...

...Twelve ... thirteen ... fourteen ... then Justin couldn't take another step, because the tree stood in his path. It stood on the very spot where he had buried the sock the night before.

It was a very beautiful plant, different to any tree Justin had ever seen before. There were no flowers on it, only leaves, rich green in colour with a silvery glow at their edges.

Perhaps Miss Morgan might recognize the leaves, and tell me what kind of a tree it is, thought Justin. Miss Morgan, his teacher, loved teaching her Year 3 and 4 class about the wonders of nature. By now, Justin was kicking himself for not listening more carefully in her lessons when she talked about the leaves of different trees.

He decided he would take one leaf to school to show her, hoping that she could help him solve the mystery of this unknown shrub. Carefully, he held one of the small twigs, and with his other hand, pinched a leaf free.

What happened next was incredible. The leaf turned into a five-pound note before his eyes! *What on earth was happening?!*

'JUUUUSTIIIIN!' Startled by the sound of his mother's angry voice, Justin stuffed the money in his pocket. His mother was shouting at him through her bedroom window!

'That alarm clock is making a racket in your bedroom, and if you don't turn it off this minute, you and your clock will have to look for somewhere else to live!'

'Sorry, Mam!' replied Justin, his voice trembling, and he ran upstairs to switch the alarm clock off.

*   *   *

Justin sat on his bed. His heart was beating like a drum just thinking about the strange thing that had just happened in the garden. Had he imagined it all? Maybe he'd been sleepwalking? He reached his hand into his pocket. There was definitely a piece of paper there. He took it out carefully. Yes. It was a five-pound note. He lifted the paper money up against the light, holding it towards the window. Yes, he could see the queen's face on it, frowning back at him. Justin shook his head. He couldn't understand, or believe, what he had seen. Did he actually have money growing on a tree ... in his garden?!

6

Justin didn't have much luck in focusing on his lessons in school all day. How was he expected to answer Miss Morgan's questions about the Tudors, when he had tens of thousands of questions to answer in his own head?

If one leaf had turned into a fiver when it was removed from the tree, would the rest do the same? And if he had a hundred leaves on the tree ... that would make him a very rich boy! Would new leaves grow instead of the leaves that were removed? If so, he could remove all the leaves tonight and find it full of leaves again tomorrow. Then, he could double the money! He would be a millionaire in no time!

Justin hadn't had the opportunity yet to explore the amazing new tree in more detail because his mum had been watching him like a hawk. She had certainly got out of bed on the wrong side that morning. Her mood was terrible following the unfortunate incident of the alarm clock. She couldn't get Justin out of the house fast enough, so that she could go back to her cosy bed.

'Justin Jones! Have you listened to a word of this discussion?' Another question from Miss Morgan.

'I'm sorry, Miss Morgan. I was ... doing ... some mental maths.' At least no one could accuse him of lying!

'Let's leave that to the maths lesson tomorrow, Justin and focus on history for the remaining two minutes of the day.'

'I'm sorry, Miss Morgan,' said Justin obediently. He hadn't intended to be rude, or not pay attention to his teacher. After all, concentrating during his lessons was very important to him, because he had his dream that one day, he would be successful.

But ... having said that, he also had money growing on a tree in his back garden. Did he really need much more than that to succeed? Perhaps, in years to come, children would be studying *him* in history lessons at school!

*   *   *

DING DING!

'Well, well,' thought Simon Shop Around. Business was obviously on the up, with the doorbell ringing for the second day in a row. If he could actually get the customer to buy something, it would be even better.

His heart sank when he saw the boy with the crow's nest of a haircut standing at the door, the same one who had taunted him yesterday.

'Oh. You. I have nothing to sell to you here,' he said abruptly.

'Yes you do,' disagreed Justin, before adding, '*Wow Words!* The dictionary!'

Although he felt sure that his life could easily be successful just with the help of his wonderful money tree, Justin decided that he would drop by Shop Around to buy the dictionary anyway, simply because he could.

'Do you think I was born yesterday?' Simon raised his voice.

'Of course not,' replied Justin politely, before adding, 'You look way too old to have been born yesterday.'

'Huh! Children!' muttered Simon. 'When I was your age …'

Here we go, thought Justin, that same old sentence again. He decided that the best way to change the subject would be by placing his hand (with the five-pound note in it) on the shop counter.

'I have some money. Can I buy *Wow Words!* please?'

Simon looked down his round nose on the banknote, before snatching it and holding it towards the light. Yes, it was real money sure enough.

'I'm afraid you don't have enough money,' said Simon, after a moment. 'The dictionary costs eight pounds.'

'But there's a 50% discount on it!' Justin corrected him.

'That was yesterday. For one day only. Today, it is sold only for the full amount, and you don't have enough money to buy it.'

'But I have more money,' insisted Justin. 'I'll be back before long to buy it!'

And off he went through the door, full of enthusiasm as he had been the day before. But this time he heard Simon's impatient voice calling, 'That's what you said yesterday!'

Justin was halfway down the street by the time Simon had finished his sentence. So, he didn't notice the pound coin lying clearly in the middle of the pavement, or his foot landing on it as he ran as fast as he could towards home.

7

'Please, please, please turn into a fiver!' prayed Justin silently as he rubbed a single leaf on the tree, between his finger and thumb. If the other leaves weren't going to turn into money, he would have to face a difficult decision. Did he want the dictionary so badly that he would dig to get the £1.02 from the ground? At least he would then be nearer his goal of getting the dictionary. Or would that be likely to destroy any hope of getting more money from the tree, once and for all?

'Please, please, please ...' Justin closed his eyes and pinched the leaf loose from the twig. Very, very slowly, he peered through half-closed eyes, before opening them wide in surprise. A smile spread across his face. Another five pounds! This was so easy. He grabbed another leaf, and another one, and continued until he had ten five-pound notes in the palm of his hand. Then he realized that he had better hurry back to the shop before it closed. Even more importantly, he had to disappear before his mum heard that he was home. He certainly didn't want her to ruin everything for him again.

Justin went back towards Shop Around, rushing past the bus stop where a group of boys from his school had gathered. He could hear them mocking him as he strode past.

'Hey, look boys, Justin is 'just-in' so much of a hurry' to get somewhere!'

The rest laughed.

'Get on your way, Justin The-Way!' said another one, followed by a big cheer from everyone.

Justin ignored them. Or tried to ignore them anyway. It was impossible not to listen to their words, but he had learnt by now how not to respond, so that the bullies thought that either he hadn't heard or that the words didn't hurt him.

*   *   *

After trying every button on the till's top row, Simon gave the big blue button on the bottom row a go, but without luck. He just couldn't remember how to open the drawer to put money in it.

'I won't be two minutes,' he told his young customer, whose nose was already in his new dictionary. Simon wiped the sweat off of his forehead with a floral handkerchief, before stuffing it back up his sleeve for safekeeping.

This task was giving him such a headache. The boy had run away from him twice in the last two days, and he certainly wasn't going to let the little monkey get the better of him again. He began pressing each button in the second row in turn.

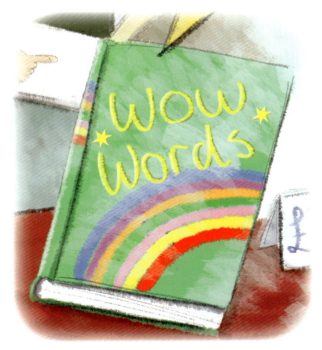

Justin hugged his new purchase. Finally, he had the book he had been dreaming of owning. *Wow Words!* He would surely win every Spelling Bee competition in school now with this new book, full of new words. Who knew, he thought, maybe that would make him popular among the other children in his class?

PING! The till rang in quite a flat tone, as if waking from a deep sleep.

'Thank goodness for that,' said Simon, before taking the two five-pound notes and gathering up the correct change which was due to the boy. Justin stuffed the coins in his left pocket.

'Oh, and while I'm here,' said Justin, 'do you sell any felt pens for left-handed people?'

'Hmmm,' Simon thought long and hard. 'I'll just go to the storeroom to check.' Then he disappeared through the door behind the counter.

Simon was so busy rummaging through the shelves in the storeroom for left-handed felt pens that he didn't hear his customer sneaking out of the shop, sniggering. Three quarters of an hour later, the shopkeeper realized that he had been made a fool of, yet again!

8

Much to Justin's surprise, none of the boys shouted at
him as he walked towards the bus stop on his way home
for the second time that afternoon. They did not laugh;
there was no cruel name-calling; they weren't even
looking at him, and so he walked past trying to appear
as confident as possible, with his head held high. A little
too high, unfortunately, so he didn't see one of the boys
stretching out his leg, causing him to trip and fall to the
ground. The boys laughed.

'Just in the way again, Justin The-Way!'

'What on earth is this?' One of them had noticed
the dictionary.

'Is this why you were you in such a hurry?
Because you wanted to go to the library to borrow a

dictionary!'

That led to more laughter, along with words like 'Pathetic!' and 'Sad!' from their nasty mouths.

'But I haven't borrowed it, I've bought it. From a shop,' explained Justin, getting back to his feet.

There was a moment of silence as the gang stared at him, completely bemused by this, then laughed again.

'That's even worse!' said the gang's ring leader. 'Couldn't you think of something better to spend your money on?'

'Yeah, like a haircut?' offered the tallest of the bunch before laughing out loud at his own joke. 'You've been wearing the same jumper since you were in Year 2, right? The bottoms of your trousers are halfway up to your knees and your shoes are full of holes. And you go and buy ... a *dictionary*?!'

They were staring at poor Justin as if the dictionary had grown like a horn on his forehead.

'You really are a bit weird, Justin,' said the leader. But for a moment, he had a look in his eyes as if he almost felt sorry for Justin. 'Come on, lads.' And the rest followed him like sheep up the street.

Justin bent down to pick his dictionary up off the ground. As he did so, he couldn't help looking at his feet. The boys were right – his shoes were in a right state. Perhaps he would be more likely to be accepted by everyone else if he wore neater and trendier

footwear? He remembered the money he had, burning
a hole in his pocket, and turned to look at the row
of shops on the other side of the street. One shop in
particular caught his attention. Towering confidently
between the 'Bread of Heaven' bakery and Flora's
Flowers was the town's best shoe shop, SOLE'D.

   Having nothing to lose, he strolled across the
road and into the shop.
   He walked slowly along a row of shelves looking
at the variety on offer. A black school shoe. A brown
school shoe. A yellow work shoe. A white trainer. A blue
trainer ... Shoe after shoe after shoe.
   'Can I help you?' asked a kind voice behind him.

Justin turned to find that the face matched the lovely voice perfectly, with a broad warm smile showing off a row of perfectly white teeth. He couldn't remember the last time someone had treated him this kindly. He was so busy thinking about this, that he forgot to answer the lady. So, she tried asking again if he wanted any help.

'Have you seen a particular shoe that you like?'

'Oh yes,' replied Justin enthusiastically. 'I've seen a lot of nice ones. But ... the thing is ... I'm looking for two.'

'I'm sorry?' asked the lady, obviously quite confused.

'I need two – one for the right foot and one for the left. So far, I've only seen shoes for one foot.'

He was a little bit hurt to see the woman laughing at him. She sensed this, so she stopped laughing and began to explain more clearly, 'Every shoe you see on the shelves here has a partner in our storeroom. They all come in pairs.'

'Oh, right, I see,' said Justin, feeling himself blushing. 'If so, could I try these?' He asked, pointing to the brightest, flashiest trainers in the shop.

'Of course you can, young man,' replied the woman, 'What size?'

'The same size as these, please,' said Justin, taking off his old, worn shoes, and offering them to the lady.

9

Justin felt like a completely different person in his light, bright and fashionable brand new trainers. It was much easier to walk energetically in these than in his old shoes. With each step he took, he felt as if he was walking on the moon. They had certainly been worth every penny he had in his pocket – however much that was. He didn't care about a few pounds here or there any more, especially now he had grown his personal 'bank' in the garden!

He had great plans for many things. How to

spend the money in order to look better. How he was going to attract friends by offering to buy things for them. And if that failed, he could even buy himself a puppy to be his good and loyal friend. What he hadn't planned, however, was how he was going to explain these new goods to his mother.

*   *   *

At home later, and within fifteen minutes of being sent to his bedroom by his furious Mam, Justin heard a knock on the front door. They hardly ever had visitors to the house, but when they did, no one ever used the front door.

'JUSTIN!' called his mother. 'Come down to the lounge, right now!' As usual, she did not sound happy.

As he walked towards the lounge, Justin could see his mother through the open door, sitting on the sofa. She was talking to someone. 'Aunty Brenda perhaps,' Justin thought at first, but then he heard a man's voice ... and the voice of a female stranger. He stepped, sheepishly, into the kitchen. He wasn't expecting to see the scene in front of him at all.

Oh no! Justin swallowed hard. He had never imagined his mother would have reacted like this, and called the police! Because that was who the two strangers were.

'Here he is, the little thief,' she said in a surly

voice.

'I'm sorry, Mrs Jones,' said the lady police officer, looking over her hasty notes, 'but I'm not quite sure what you're telling us.'

'It's completely obvious,' insisted his mum, 'the boy has been stealing.'

'But, Mam ...' Justin tried to explain – but he wasn't given a chance.

She continued angrily. 'Now, people in this town can call us whatever they want, but they will *not* call us thieves. I've bought this boy up to know better, and I want him to learn his lesson, so you can deal with him now.'

'Right then, Justin,' said the policeman, calmly. 'Your mother says you arrived home from school this afternoon wearing a brand new pair of trainers. Is this ...'

'... and with a new book too!' added his mother.

'Thank you, Mrs Jones,' said the policeman, impatiently, before turning his attention back to Justin. 'Is this true?'

Justin nodded, staring at a hard crust under the policeman's chair.

'Where did you get these swish shoes from, Justin?' asked the female police officer.

'And the book!' Mam poked her nose into the conversation once again.

'Mrs Jones, please,' said the policeman, more

firmly this time. 'We are trying to ask your son some questions so we can answer your concerns. So, we would appreciate it if you let Justin answer. It might be better for us to talk to him on his own?'

Mrs Jones got up, mumbling something about 'telling me what to do ... in my own home'. Then she

slammed the door shut after her.

Justin saw the police officers looking at each other, with raised eyebrows, before they turned back to look at him. One police officer leaned forward in her chair. She smiled.

'I like your new shoes, Justin. Very smart.'

'Yes,' agreed the man. 'I wonder if they make them in my size.'

'Oh, yes,' replied Justin. 'They have some for feet of all sizes in SOLE'D!'

Both police officers smiled. It was clear that the boy had been to a shop to get them, anyway. Their work would be very simple from now on. It was just a matter of looking at the CCTV cameras in the shop now to see whether the boy had bought them, or stolen them.

'And what about the book? Where did you get that from?' asked the woman.

'Shop Around,' Justin replied firmly.

'I wonder if they have CCTV cameras there?' wondered the policeman. 'Highly unlikely.'

'Thank you, Justin, for your time,' said one police officer as they both stood up.

He sighed in relief as he realised they were about to leave, and that it had all been much easier than he had expected.

Before reaching the door, the lady turned to look at him and asked, 'Is there anything else you'd like to tell us, Justin? Before we go?'

Justin thought hard. It would probably be best for him to keep his mouth shut, but he wanted them to know that he hadn't done anything wrong. He wondered what would happen if he told them about the tree in the garden. After all, they couldn't take it off him, because it was his tree. He'd planted it.

'I ...' he ventured, before closing his mouth again.

'Yes?' The police officer spoke softly, with a kind look on her face.

'I haven't stolen anything,' he said, looking straight into the police officer's eyes. 'Honestly. I paid for them – the shoes and the book!'

'Liar!' The police officers were almost hit by the door as it was swung open. Justin's mother had obviously been standing with one ear to the door since she'd left the room.

'Last night, you were crying like a baby because you didn't have a penny to your name. So, how could you afford to buy shoes and a book today?' Her voice was strong and harsh.

Justin couldn't answer. He certainly couldn't tell his mother about the amazing tree. But, as luck would have it, he didn't have to say anything because the police stepped in.

'Leave this to us, Mrs Jones. We will make further inquiries. Could we have a private word, please?'

His mother looked fiercely at Justin, before tidying up her hair, straightening her back and saying, 'Of course, Sergeant. This way.'

And she swept out like a whirlwind, the police officers following her, shaking their heads.

10

Justin had a lot of explaining to do to his mother, and he didn't have a clue where to start. The police had contacted her later that evening. They had told her that they had solid evidence to confirm that neither the shoes nor the dictionary had been stolen. She insisted that Justin must have stolen the money then. The police's reply was that no one had reported a theft in the area. They had contacted the school, but no money had been lost there either. She had nothing to worry about, according to the police.

However, she wanted some answers from him.

'I had more money ... saved ... somewhere else,' Justin tried to explain.

This wasn't a lie, but nevertheless he could not look at his mother, who stood over him, with a frown on her face and her arms crossed.

'Are you trying to tell me,' she began her lecture, 'that you've been watching me struggling to make ends meet in this house – barely managing to get enough money to put food on the table, while you were hiding a fortune from me?!'

No answer came from Justin.

'What were you expecting to have for supper tonight, Justin? Did you expect a meal to appear on the table? Do you think that there's an endless stock of food in these cupboards?'

'I have some money left over, Mam. Enough to buy a bag of chips for us both.'

'GET OUT OF MY SIGHT!' exploded his mother.

And Justin disappeared through the back door. He didn't go far. Not far at all. Only as far as the back garden. He knew the situation would only go from bad to worse if he strayed further than that.

BANG! BANG! BANG! His mother was making a racket in the kitchen, opening the food cupboard doors then slamming them shut again.

Justin grabbed his chance to study the tree. There were fewer leaves on it than he expected. He must have removed half of them before going to the shop, because there were only ten leaves left. But he noticed that new leaves had started sprouting to replace those he had taken.

That meant (it was time for mental maths again!) if there were twenty leaves on the tree, each leaf giving him a fiver, he could get …

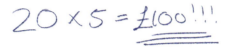

ONE HUNDRED POUNDS A DAY! And if the buds developed into new leaves by tomorrow – TWO HUNDRED POUNDS! How much would he have in a week? How much in two weeks? How many days would it take him to have a thousand pounds in his pockets?

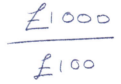

The back door opened, and his mother shouted at him. 'JUSTIN!'

'Yes, Mam?' he replied, expecting the worst.

'Go and get those chips, if you say you have some money left. I'm starving.'

'Okay, Mam,' said Justin obediently, before she slammed the back door shut again.

Justin took every single leaf left off the tree. He stuffed them quickly into his pocket in case his mother happened to look out of the window and see them change into money. He wasn't expecting the chips to cost that much, of course, but he had an idea. By removing all the leaves, new ones would sprout and grow by the next day. That would allow him to save more money, faster.

Justin wanted to buy a new house for himself, so that he wouldn't have to endure living with his mother for much longer.

So, on his way to Chiptastic, the local fish and chip shop, Justin paused to look at the window display of an estate agent's shop on the street. There were loads of houses for sale in the town. Justin loved one house immediately – it was huge! Then he noticed that they wanted a huge price for it too. Even the smaller houses had too many '0s' in the price. Justin would have to pick leaves for years before being able to afford a home. But, he was ready for the challenge.

GROOOOOWL! The strangest sound came from his stomach. Justin was starving, so he followed the smell of chips towards Chiptastic. He was so hungry, he didn't notice the twenty pence piece on the doorstep.

11

CHIPTASTIC

Large chips	£1.50	Baked beans	60p
Small chips	£1.20	Mushy peas	65p
Fish	£2.20	Ketchup	10p
Pie	£1.50	Bottled pop	75p
Sausage	£1.30		

Justin could have bought all the chips in the shop with the money he had in his pocket, probably. But he had to spend carefully. He certainly didn't want his mother to get suspicious again.

As he eyed the menu on the wall, he licked his lips. The smell was mouth-watering. A man with a big moustache stood on the other side of the counter, wearing a striped apron to hide his belly. He was busy lifting chips from the oil, and tossing them into another compartment of sizzling fat.

'What can I get you, boy?' asked the pot-bellied

man, continuing his work without even looking at his customer.

'Could I have a big bag of chips, please?' asked Justin politely.

'No problem, boy. That'll be one pound and fifty pence.'

'A bargain!' thought Justin, and with that he added, 'Can I also have a fish in a separate package ... and sausage ... and mushy peas.'

'Anything else?' said the mouth behind the moustache.

'A bottle of pop ... and some tomato ketchup, please.'

The man couldn't do that sum. So he went to the till and pressed the prices into it, so that the machine did the hard work for him. Justin gave him two five-pounds notes, thanked him for his change and headed towards home.

But Justin didn't go straight home. He decided to stay in the park to eat his fish alone in peace, and the sausage (with ketchup), along with the mushy peas, and then washed it all down with the drink.

BURP! Justin hadn't had a feast like that in a long time! And it wasn't finished yet either. He had a big bag of chips to share with his mother once he got home. There was no need for her to know about the fish, the sausage or the mushy peas, of course. But his hands were very greasy and he had a big dollop of ketchup on his trousers.

He rummaged through his pockets for a tissue. He didn't have one, of course. The only thing he had was a pocket full of five-pound notes. He supposed that he wouldn't miss one of them, so he took one and used it to scrape the ketchup off his trousers carefully. Then

he folded the paper and used the same fiver to dry his greasy hands. He threw the money into the bin and walked home, hoping that the chips hadn't gone too cold.

*   *   *

Justin slept well that night after such a chaotic (but exciting) day, followed by a bellyful of food. As soon as his head landed on his pillow, he fell asleep with a smile on his face. He knew that today was the first day of the rest of his life.

12

The following morning, just like every other morning, Justin's mother was shouting at him. This time, however, she was shouting at him to wake up.

'JUSTIIIIIIIN! WAKE UP! Or you'll be late for school!'

In his excitement, or tiredness the night before, he'd forgotten to set his alarm clock for the morning. He scrambled out of bed to the bathroom, and from the bathroom back to his bedroom. Dressing hurriedly, he ran downstairs to the kitchen, reached for his coat, wore his new shoes and went out through the door. He paused there for a moment, long enough to see the amazing tree covered with green leaves again.

He smiled, then ran to school.

*　　*　　*

His day at school day went by easily enough, although very slowly. At lunchtime, he was surprised to discover that the same boys who had been making fun of his old, tatty shoes were now mocking him for his new shoes. Maybe they laughed because they were too bright, too dazzling or too clean. It was most likely that they were laughing just because they were on Justin's feet.

But he had more important things to worry about. For example ... where was he going to hide his new fortune? Perhaps he could bury his next fortune underground too. If he placed two five-pound notes in a sock in the ground, would the leaves on that tree become ten-pound notes? Or twenty-pound notes? Perhaps he could plant a row of money trees? Or even a whole forest?

Justin had also considered admitting the truth to his mum, by telling her about the tree. Perhaps she would be happier knowing that there was no need for them to worry about money any more. Perhaps that would make her like him more, and make them friends? Who could tell?

On his way home from school, he was tempted to go shopping to look for something to buy with the left over money that was burning a hole in his pocket since the day before. But he decided it would be better not to. He certainly didn't want the police calling by his house again. So he went straight home.

Before he'd even opened the back door, Justin could hear his mother singing loudly from the living room, 'La, la, la, la ...', and clapping her hands slightly behind the beat of the music on the radio. This was his chance, Justin thought. While she was in a good mood and hadn't realised that he was home, he could collect the new leaves off the tree!

He walked towards the plant, rubbing his hands together, excited and eager. He glanced over his shoulder again, to make sure that his mother wasn't watching him. Then he took the first leaf from the twig and stuffed it in his pocket.

He was about to remove the second leaf straight away when he realized that something was very different. The first leaf he'd picked had filled his pocket completely. And it didn't tickle his leg through the pocket lining like the banknotes had done the day before either. It felt slightly heavier too. He put his hand in his pocket, only to feel a material very different to paper. This was more like wool. He took it out carefully to see what it was.

A sock! No! Justin threw it to the ground and pulled a second leaf from the tree. This time, he watched the leaf changing in front of his eye. It began to stretch and turn into a green sock. Justin dropped it on the floor and took another leaf, and another one, and another, to see each one turning into green socks.

He couldn't believe it. He'd been so sure that the new leaves would bring more money. He didn't need more socks!

When Justin pulled the last leaf loose from the

twig, the tree disappeared completely. There was no trace of it ever having been there at all!

Justin fell to his knees. He couldn't believe it! He started digging with his hands in the place where the tree had been standing a few seconds earlier. But there was no sign of the sock he'd buried, or the £1.02.

'Justin The-Way Jones! What on earth are you doing?' his mother's voice rolled like thunder through the garden. Justin didn't have the energy or the heart to answer.

'Who do you think you are? Next door's dog?' She couldn't believe the scene in front of her eyes, so she came closer to see what her son was doing. 'And what in the world are you doing with all these socks?!'

Afterword

Acceptable ... Adequate ... Admirable ... Adventurous ... Amazing ... Amusing ... Awesome.

A fortnight later, Justin had several excellent adjectives to describe his journey home from school. And he'd only got as far as section 'A' of Wow Words! Walking along the main street alone, he'd found a pound coin shining in the sun in the middle of the pavement by Shop Around. Then, he came across a twenty pence piece on Chiptastic's doorstep. To top it all, he spotted a grubby looking fiver caught in between some twigs in the park's hedge.

'Some people are so careless with their money!' thought Justin, before heading for home, to read section 'B' of Wow Words!

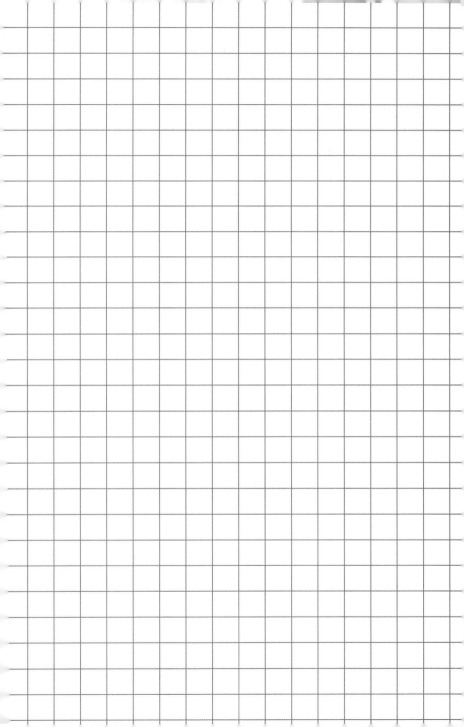

Money
Matters

Also in the series

978-1-78390-070-1

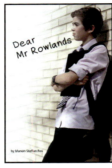

978-1-78390-071-8

978-1-78390-068-8

In addition to the novels, the series has a designated website for readers that includes interactive activities which provide further opportunities for readers to consider the financial situations that occur within the text.

For more information, go to
www.canolfanpeniarth.org/moneymatters